Q9

BIRD, BEAST AND FLOWER

BIRD, BEAST AND FLOWER

With Watercolours by

MARIE ANGEL

And Poems chosen by

IAN PARSONS

CHATTO & WINDUS · LONDON

Published by
Chatto & Windus Ltd
40 William IV Street
London WC2N 4DF

*

Clarke, Irwin and Co Ltd
Toronto

British Library Cataloguing in Publication Data
Bird, beast and flower.
    1. English Poetry – 20th century
    I. Angel, Marie   II. Parsons, Ian
    821'.9'1408   PR1225
    ISBN 0-7011-2411-3

Acknowledgments for the use of copyright
material will be found on page 64
which are hereby made part of this copyright page

Watercolours © Marie Angel 1980
Selection and Arrangement © Chatto & Windus 1980

Printed in Great Britain by Westerham Press Ltd

Alphabetical List of Authors and Poems

A Guide to the Illustrations

BIRD, BEAST AND FLOWER

THE TIGER

Tiger! tiger! burning bright
In the forests of the night,
What immortal hand or eye
Could frame thy fearful symmetry?

In what distant deeps or skies
Burnt the fire of thine eyes?
On what wings dare he aspire?
What the hand dare seize the fire?

And what shoulder, and what art,
Could twist the sinews of thy heart?
And, when thy heart began to beat,
What dread hand? and what dread feet?

What the hammer? What the chain?
In what furnace was thy brain?
What the anvil? What dread grasp
Dare its deadly terrors clasp?

When the stars threw down their spears,
And water'd heaven with their tears,
Did He smile His work to see?
Did He who made the lamb make thee?

Tiger! tiger! burning bright
In the forests of the night,
What immortal hand or eye
Dare frame thy fearful symmetry?

WILLIAM BLAKE

A NARROW FELLOW

A narrow fellow in the grass
Occasionally rides;
You may have met him, – did you not?
His notice sudden is.

The grass divides as with a comb,
A spotted shaft is seen;
And then it closes at your feet
And opens further on.

He likes a boggy acre,
A floor too cool for corn.
Yet when a child, and barefoot,
I more than once, at morn,

Have passed, I thought, a whip-lash
Unbraiding in the sun, –
When, stooping to secure it,
It wrinkled, and was gone.

Several of nature's people
I know, and they know me;
I feel for them a transport
Of cordiality;

But never met this fellow,
Attended or alone,
Without a tighter breathing,
And zero at the bone.

EMILY DICKINSON

FABLE

The mountain and the squirrel
Had a quarrel,
And the former called the latter 'Little Prig';
Bun replied,
'You are doubtless very big;
But all sorts of things and weather
Must be taken in together,
To make up a year
And a sphere.
And I think it no disgrace
To occupy my place.
If I'm not so large as you,
You are not so small as I,
And not half so spry.
I'll not deny you make
A very pretty squirrel track;
Talents differ; all is well and wisely put;
If I cannot carry forests on my back,
Neither can you crack a nut.'

RALPH WALDO EMERSON

From IN MEMORIAM

Unwatch'd, the garden bough shall sway,
    The tender blossom flutter down,
    Unloved, that beech will gather brown,
This maple burn itself away;

Unloved, the sunflower, shining fair,
    Ray round with flames her disk of seed,
    And many a rose-carnation feed
With summer spice the humming air;

Unloved, by many a sandy bar,
    The brook shall babble down the plain,
    At noon or when the lesser wain
Is twisting round the polar star;

Uncared for, gird the windy grove,
    And flood the haunts of hern and crake;
    Or into silver arrows break
The sailing moon in creek and cove;

Till from the garden and the wild
    A fresh association blow,
    And year by year the landscape grow
Familiar to the stranger's child;

As year by year the labourer tills
    His wonted glebe, or lops the glades;
    And year by year our memory fades
From all the circle of the hills.

ALFRED TENNYSON

BRIDAL SONG

Roses, their sharp spines being gone,
    Not royal in their smells alone,
But in their hue;
Maiden pinks, of odour faint,
Daisies smell-less, yet most quaint,
    And sweet thyme true;

Primrose, firstborn child of Ver;
Merry springtime's harbinger,
    With harebells dim;
Oxlips in their cradles growing,
Marigolds on death-beds blowing,
    Larks'-heels trim;

All dear Nature's children sweet
Lie 'fore bride and bridegroom's feet,
    Blessing their sense!
Not an angel of the air,
Bird melodious or bird fair,
    Be absent hence!

The crow, the slanderous cuckoo, nor
The boding raven, nor chough hoar,
    Nor chattering pye,
May on our bride-house perch or sing,
Or with them any discord bring,
    But from it fly!

? JOHN FLETCHER

From **L**OVE'S LABOUR'S LOST

When daisies pied and violets blue,
    And lady-smocks all silver-white,
And cuckoo-buds of yellow hue
    Do paint the meadows with delight,
The cuckoo then, on every tree,
Mocks married men; for thus sings he,
      Cuckoo!
Cuckoo, cuckoo! – O word of fear,
Unpleasing to a married ear!

When shepherds pipe on oaten straws,
    And merry larks are ploughmen's clocks,
When turtles tread, and rooks, and daws,
    And maidens bleach their summer smocks,
The cuckoo then, on every tree,
Mocks married men; for thus sings he,
      Cuckoo!
Cuckoo, cuckoo! – O word of fear,
Unpleasing to a married ear!

WILLIAM SHAKESPEARE

TO A MOUSE

On turning her up in her nest with the plough,
November 1785

Wee, sleekit, cow'rin', tim'rous beastie,
O what a panic's in thy breastie!
Thou need na start awa sae hasty,
Wi' bickering brattle!
I wad be laith to rin an' chase thee
Wi' murd'ring pattle!

I'm truly sorry man's dominion
Has broken nature's social union,
An' justifies that ill opinion
Which makes thee startle
At me, thy poor earth-born companion,
An' fellow-mortal!

I doubt na, whiles, but thou may thieve;
What then? poor beastie, thou maun live!
A daimen-icker in a thrave
'S a sma' request:
I'll get a blessin' wi' the lave,
And never miss't.

Thy wee bit housie, too, in ruin!
Its silly wa's the win's are strewin'
An' naething, now, to big a new ane,
O' foggage green!
An' bleak December's winds ensuin'
Baith snell an' keen!

Thou saw the fields laid bare an' waste
An' weary winter comin' fast,
An' cozie here, beneath the blast,
Thou thought to dwell,
Till, crash! the cruel coulter past
Out thro' thy cell.

That wee bit heap o' leaves an' stibble
Has cost thee mony a weary nibble!
Now thou's turn'd out, for a' thy trouble,
But house or hald,
To thole the winter's sleety dribble
An' cranreuch cauld!

But, Mousie, thou art no thy lane
In proving foresight may be vain:
The best laid schemes o' mice an' men
Gang aft a-gley,
An' lea'e us nought but grief an' pain,
For promised joy.

Still thou art blest, compared wi' me!
The present only toucheth thee:
But, och! I backward cast my e'e
On prospects drear!
An' forward, tho' I canna see,
I guess an' fear!

ROBERT BURNS

19

DAY-DREAMS

Broad August burns in milky skies,
    The world is blanched with hazy heat;
The vast green pasture, even, lies
    Too hot and bright for eyes and feet.

Amid the grassy levels rears
    The sycamore against the sun
The dark boughs of a hundred years,
    The emerald foliage of one.

Lulled in a dream of shade and sheen,
    With the clement twilight thrown
By that great cloud of floating green,
    A horse is standing, still as stone.

He stirs nor head nor hoof, although
    The grass is fresh beneath the branch;
His tail alone swings to and fro
    In graceful curves from haunch to haunch.

He stands quite lost, indifferent
    To rock or pasture, trace or rein;
He feels the vaguely sweet content
    Of perfect sloth in limb and brain.

WILLIAM CANTON

THE MARCH BEE

A warning wind finds out my resting-place
And in a mountain cloud the lost sun chills;
Night comes; and yet before she shows her face
The sun flings off the shadows, warm light fills
The valley and the clearings on the hills.
Bleak crow the moorcocks on the fen's blue plashes,
But here I warm myself with these bright looks and flashes.

And warmed like me the merry humble-bee
Puts fear aside, runs forth to catch the sun,
And by the ploughland's shoulder comes to see
The flowers that like him best, and seems to shun
Cold countless quaking wind-flowers every one,
Primroses too; but makes poor grass his choice
Where small wood-strawberry blossoms nestle and rejoice.

The magpies steering round from wood to wood,
Tree-creeper flickering up the elm's green rind,
Bold gnats that revel round my solitude
And most this pleasant bee intent to find
The new-born joy, inveigle the rich mind
Long after darkness comes cold-lipped to one
Still listening to the bee, still basking in the sun.

EDMUND BLUNDEN

THE ANSWER IS 'NO'

What answer maketh the crow?
Always 'No.'

Put several questions in a row
To a crow,
You will get 'No, no, no,'
Or 'No, no, no, no.'

Sometimes on being questioned,
The crows say 'Naw'
Or 'Caw.'
But regardless of pronunciation,
There is never anything but opposition, denial,
And negation
In a crow.

In their assemblies at the edge of town,
Crows introduce resolutions, then vote them down.
How many times in summer, waked early by the mosquito,
Have I lain listening to the crow's loud veto!

Once, gunning, I wounded a thieving
Crow
And have not forgotten his terrible, disbelieving
'Oh, *no!*'

E. B. WHITE

SONG

Ask me no more where Jove bestows,
When June is past, the fading rose:
For in your beauty's orient deep
These flowers, as in their causes, sleep.

Ask me no more whither do stray
The golden atoms of the day:
For in pure love Heaven did prepare
Those powders to enrich your hair.

Ask me no more whither doth haste
The Nightingale when May is past:
For in your sweet dividing throat
She winters and keeps warm her note.

Ask me no more where those stars light
That downwards fall in dead of night:
For in your eyes they sit, and there
Fixed become as in their sphere.

Ask me no more if east or west
The Phoenix builds her spicy nest:
For unto you at last she flies,
And in your fragrant bosom dies.

THOMAS CAREW

A DREAM

Once a dream did weave a shade
O'er my Angel-guarded bed,
That an emmet lost its way
Where on grass methought I lay.

Troubled, 'wilder'd, and forlorn,
Dark, benighted, travel-worn,
Over many a tangled spray,
All heart-broke I heard her say:

'O my children! do they cry?
Do they hear their father sigh?
Now they look abroad to see:
Now return and weep for me.'

Pitying, I dropp'd a tear;
But I saw a glow-worm near,
Who replied: 'What wailing wight
Calls the watchman of the night?

'I am set to light the ground,
While the beetle goes his round:
Follow now the beetle's hum;
Little wanderer, hie thee home.'

WILLIAM BLAKE

ALL NATURE SEEMS AT WORK

All Nature seems at work. Slugs leave their lair—
The bees are stirring — birds are on the wing —
And Winter, slumbering in the open air,
Wears on his smiling face a dream of Spring!

S. T. COLERIDGE

YOU SPOTTED SNAKES

You spotted snakes, with double tongue,
    Thorny hedgehogs, be not seen;
Newts and blind-worms, do no wrong;
    Come not near our fairy queen.

Weaving spiders, come not here;
    Hence, you long-legg'd spinners, hence!
Beetles black, approach not near;
    Worm nor snail, do no offence.

      Philomel, with melody,
      Sing in our sweet lullaby;
Lulla, lulla, lullaby; lulla, lulla, lullaby!
      Never harm,
      Nor spell nor charm,
Come our lovely lady nigh;
So, good night, with lullaby.

WILLIAM SHAKESPEARE

PIPPA'S SONG

The year's at the spring,
And day's at the morn;
Morning's at seven;
The hill-side's dew-pearled;
The lark's on the wing;
The snail's on the thorn;
God's in His heaven —
All's right with the world!

ROBERT BROWNING

I WANDERED LONELY AS A CLOUD

I wandered lonely as a cloud
That floats on high o'er vales and hills,
When all at once I saw a crowd,
A host, of golden daffodils;
Beside the lake, beneath the trees,
Fluttering and dancing in the breeze.

Continuous as the stars that shine
And twinkle on the milky way,
They stretched in never-ending line
Along the margin of a bay:
Ten thousand saw I at a glance,
Tossing their heads in sprightly dance.

The waves beside them danced; but they
Out-did the sparkling waves in glee:
A poet could not but be gay,
In such a jocund company:
I gazed – and gazed – but little thought
What wealth the show to me had brought.

For oft, when on my couch I lie
In vacant or in pensive mood,
They flash upon that inward eye
Which is the bliss of solitude;
And then my heart with pleasure fills,
And dances with the daffodils.

WILLIAM WORDSWORTH

O N A BANK AS I SAT FISHING

And now all Nature seemed in love;
The lusty sap began to move;
New juice did stir the embracing vines;
And birds had drawn their Valentines:
The jealous trout, that low did lie,
Rose at a well-dissembled fly:
There stood my friend, with patient skill
Attending of his trembling quill.
Already were the eaves possessed
With the swift Pilgrim's daubéd nest.
The groves already did rejoice
In Philomel's triumphing voice.
  The showers were short, the weather mild,
The morning fresh, the evening smiled.
  Joan takes her neat-rubbed pail, and now
She trips to milk the sand-red cow;
Where for some sturdy foot-ball swain,
Joan strokes a sillabub or twain.
  The fields and gardens were beset
With Tulips, Crocus, Violet:
And now, though late, the modest Rose
Did more than half a blush disclose.
Thus all looked gay, all full of cheer,
To welcome the new-livery'd year.

SIR HENRY WOTTON

HOME THOUGHTS, FROM ABROAD

Oh, to be in England
Now that April's there,
And whoever wakes in England
Sees, some morning, unaware,
That the lowest boughs and the brushwood sheaf
Round the elm-tree bole are in tiny leaf,
While the chaffinch sings on the orchard bough
In England – now!

And after April, when May follows,
And the whitethroat builds, and all the swallows!
Hark, where my blossomed pear-tree in the hedge
Leans to the field and scatters on the clover
Blossoms and dewdrops – at the bent spray's edge –
That's the wise thrush; he sings each song twice over,
Lest you should think he never could recapture
The first fine careless rapture!
And though the fields look rough with hoary dew,
All will be gay when noontide wakes anew
The buttercups, the little children's dower
– Far brighter than this gaudy melon-flower!

ROBERT BROWNING

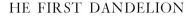

THE FIRST DANDELION

Simple and fresh and fair from winter's close emerging,
As if no artifice of fashion, business, politics, had ever been,
Forth from its sunny nook of shelter'd grass – innocent, golden,
    calm as the dawn,
The spring's first dandelion shows its trustful face.

WALT WHITMAN

FROM YOU I HAVE BEEN ABSENT

From you I have been absent in the spring,
When proud-pied April, dress'd in all his trim,
Hath put a spirit of youth in everything,
That heavy Saturn laugh'd and leap'd with him.
Yet nor the lays of birds, nor the sweet smell
Of different flowers in odour and in hue,
Could make me any summer's story tell,
Or from their proud lap pluck them where they grew;
Nor did I wonder at the Lily's white,
Nor praise the deep vermilion in the Rose;
They were but sweet, but figures of delight,
Drawn after you, you pattern of all those.
    Yet seem'd it Winter still, and, you away,
    As with your shadow I with these did play.

WILLIAM SHAKESPEARE

A BIRTHDAY

My heart is like a singing bird
    Whose nest is in a watered shoot;
My heart is like an apple-tree
    Whose boughs are bent with thickset fruit.

My heart is like a rainbow shell
    That paddles in a halcyon sea;
My heart is gladder than all these
    Because my love is come to me.

Raise me a dais of silk and down;
    Hang it with vair and purple dyes;
Carve it in doves, and pomegranates,
    And peacocks with a hundred eyes;
Work it in gold and silver grapes,
    In leaves, and silver fleurs-de-lys;
Because the birthday of my life
    Is come, my love is come to me.

CHRISTINA ROSETTI

LILIES ARE WHITE

Lilies are white,
Rosemary's green;
When you are king,
I will be queen.

Roses are red,
Lavender's blue;
If you will have me,
I will have you.

ANON

From LEAVES OF GRASS

There was a child went forth every day,
And the first object he looked upon and received with wonder or
      pity or love or dread, that object he became,
And that object became part of him for the day or a certain part of
      the day . . . or for many years or stretching cycles of years.

The early lilacs became part of this child,
And grass, and white and red morning glories, and white and red
      clover, and the song of the phoebe-bird,
And the March-born lambs, and the sow's pink-faint litter, and the
      mare's foal, and the cow's calf, and the noisy brood of the
      barnyard or by the mire of the pondside . . . and the fish
      suspending themselves so curiously below there . . . and the
      beautiful curious liquid . . . and the water-plants with their
      graceful flat heads . . . all became part of him.

And the field-sprouts of April and May became part of him . . .
      wintergrain sprouts, and those of the light-yellow corn, and of
      the esculent roots of the garden,
And the appletrees covered with blossoms, and the fruit afterward
      . . . and woodberries . . . and the commonest weeds by the road;
And the old drunkard staggering home from the outhouse of the
      tavern whence he had lately risen,
And the schoolmistress that passed on her way to the school . . . and
      the friendly boys that passed . . . and the quarrelsome boys
      . . . and the tidy and freshcheeked girls . . . and the barefoot
      negro boy and girl,
And all the changes of city and country wherever he went.

WALT WHITMAN

34

WEATHERS

This is the weather the cuckoo likes,
    And so do I;
When showers betumble the chestnut spikes,
    And nestlings fly;
And the little brown nightingale bills his best,
And they sit outside at 'The Travellers' Rest,'
And maids come forth sprig-muslin drest,
And citizens dream of the south and west,
    And so do I.

This is the weather the shepherd shuns,
    And so do I;
When beeches drip in browns and duns,
    And thresh, and ply;
And hill-hid tides throb, throe on throe,
And meadow rivulets overflow,
And drops on gate-bars hang in a row,
And rooks in families homeward go,
    And so do I.

THOMAS HARDY

SONG

The owl is abroad,
The Bat and the Toad,
And so is the Cat-a-mountain;
The Ant and the Mole
Sit both in a hole,
And the Frog peeps out of the fountain.

ANON

From **THYRSIS**

So, some tempestuous morn in early June,
When the year's primal burst of bloom is o'er,
Before the roses and the longest day –
When garden-walks, and all the grassy floor,
With blossoms, red and white, of fallen May,
And chestnut-flowers are strewn –
So have I heard the cuckoo's parting cry,
From the wet field, through the vext garden-trees,
Come with the volleying rain and tossing breeze:
The bloom is gone, and with the bloom go I.

Too quick despairer, wherefore wilt thou go?
Soon will the high Midsummer pomps come on,
Soon will the musk carnations break and swell,
Soon shall we have gold-dusted snapdragon,
Sweet-William with its homely cottage-smell,
And stocks in fragrant blow;
Roses that down the alleys shine afar,
And open, jasmine-muffled lattices,
And groups under the dreaming garden-trees,
And the full moon, and the white evening-star.

MATTHEW ARNOLD

SONNET TO A CAT

Cat! who hast pass'd thy grand climacteric,
       How many mice and rats hast in thy days
       Destroy'd? – How many tit bits stolen? Gaze
With those bright languid segments green, and prick
Those velvet ears – but pr'ythee do not stick
       Thy latent talons in me – and upraise
       Thy gentle mew – and tell me all thy frays
Of fish and mice, and rats and tender chick.
Nay, look not down, nor lick thy dainty wrists –
       For all thy wheezy asthma, – and for all
Thy tail's tip is nick'd off – and though the fists
       Of many a maid have given thee many a maul,
Still is that fur as soft as when the lists
       In youth thou enter'dst on glass bottled wall.

JOHN KEATS

CORNELIA'S SONG

Call for the Robin-Red-breast and the wren,
Since o'er shady groves they hover,
And with leaves and flowers do cover
The friendless bodies of unburied men.
Call unto his funeral Dole
The Ant, the field-mouse, and the mole
To rear him hillocks, that shall keep him warm,
And (when gay tombs are robb'd) sustain no harm,
But keep the wolf far thence, that's foe to men,
For with his nails he'll dig them up again.

JOHN WEBSTER

THE TRIUMPH OF CHARIS

See the Chariot at hand here of Love,
    Wherein my Lady rideth!
Each that draws is a swan or a dove,
    And well the car Love guideth.
As she goes, all hearts do duty
        Unto her beauty;
And enamoured do wish, so they might
        But enjoy such a sight,
That they still were to run by her side,
Through swards, through seas, whither she would ride.

Do but look on her eyes, they do light
    All that Love's world compriseth!
Do but look on her hair, it is bright
    As Love's star when it riseth!
Do but mark, her forehead's smoother
        Than words that soothe her;
And from her arched brows such a grace
        Sheds itself through the face,
As alone there triumphs to the life
All the gain, all the good, of the elements' strife.

Have you seen but a bright lily grow
    Before rude hands have touch'd it?
Have you mark'd but the fall of the snow
    Before the soil hath smutch'd it?
Have you felt the wool of beaver,
        Or swan's down ever?
Or have smelt o' the bud o' the brier,
        Or the nard in the fire?
Or have tasted the bag of the bee?
O so white, O so soft, O so sweet is she!

BEN JONSON

39

THE TUFT OF FLOWERS

I went to turn the grass once after one
Who mowed it in the dew before the sun.

The dew was gone that made his blade so keen
Before I came to view the levelled scene.

I looked for him behind an isle of trees;
I listened for his whetstone on the breeze.

But he had gone his way, the grass all mown,
And I must be, as he had been – alone,

'As all must be,' I said within my heart,
'Whether they work together or apart.'

But as I said it, swift there passed me by
On noiseless wing a bewildered butterfly,

Seeking with memories grown dim o'er night
Some resting flower of yesterday's delight.

And once I marked his flight go round and round,
As where some flower lay withering on the ground.

And then he flew as far as eye could see,
And then on tremulous wing came back to me.

I thought of questions that have no reply,
And would have turned to toss the grass to dry;

But he turned first, and led my eye to look
At a tall tuft of flowers beside a brook,

A leaping tongue of bloom the scythe had spared
Beside a reedy brook the scythe had bared.

The mower in the dew had loved them thus,
By leaving them to flourish, not for us,

Nor yet to draw one thought of ours to him.
But from sheer morning gladness at the brim.

The butterfly and I had lit upon,
Nevertheless, a message from the dawn,

That made me hear the wakening birds around,
And hear his long scythe whispering to the ground,

And feel a spirit kindred to my own;
So that henceforth I worked no more alone;

But glad with him, I worked as with his aid,
And weary, sought at noon with him the shade;

And dreaming, as it were, held brotherly speech
With one whose thought I had not hoped to reach.

'Men work together,' I told him from the heart,
'Whether they work together or apart.'

ROBERT FROST

THE OWL

When cats run home and light is come,
　And dew is cold upon the ground,
And the far-off stream is dumb,
　And the whirring sail goes round,
　And the whirring sail goes round;
　　Alone and warming his five wits,
　　The white owl in the belfry sits.

When merry milkmaids click the latch,
　And rarely smells the new-mown hay,
And the cock hath sung beneath the thatch
　Twice or thrice his roundelay,
　Twice or thrice his roundelay;
　　Alone and warming his five wits,
　　The white owl in the belfry sits.

ALFRED TENNYSON

ARIEL'S SONG

Where the bee sucks, there suck I.
In a cowslip's bell I lie.
There I couch, when owls do cry.
On the bat's back I do fly
After summer merrily . . .
Merrily, merrily, shall I live now,
Under the blossom that hangs on the bough.

WILLIAM SHAKESPEARE

From MAR KHAYYÁM

They say the Lion and the Lizard keep
The Courts where Jamshyd gloried and drank deep:
      And Bahram, that great Hunter – the wild Ass
Stamps o'er his Head, but cannot break his Sleep.

I sometimes think that never blows so red
The Rose as where some buried Caesar bled;
      That every Hyacinth the Garden wears
Dropt in her Lap from some once lovely Head.

And this reviving Herb whose tender Green
Fledges the River-Lip on which we lean –
      Ah, lean upon it lightly! for who knows
From what once lovely Lip it springs unseen!

Ah, my Belovéd, fill the Cup that clears
TO-DAY of past Regrets and Future Fears:
      To-morrow! – Why, To-morrow I may be
Myself with Yesterday's Sev'n thousand Years.

TrS. EDWARD FITZGERALD

LURIANA, LURILEE

Come out and climb the garden path
    Luriana, Lurilee.
The China rose is all abloom
And buzzing with the yellow bee.
We'll swing you on the cedar bough,
    Luriana, Lurilee.

I wonder if it seems to you,
    Luriana, Lurilee,
That all the lives we ever lived
And all the lives to be,
Are full of trees and changing leaves,
    Luriana, Lurilee.

How long it seems since you and I,
    Luriana, Lurilee,
Roamed in the forest where our kind
Had just begun to be,
And laughed and chattered in the flowers,
    Luriana, Lurilee.

How long since you and I went out,
    Luriana, Lurilee,
To see the Kings go riding by
Over lawn and daisy lea,
With their palm leaves and cedar sheaves,
    Luriana, Lurilee.

Swing, swing, on the cedar-bough,
    Luriana, Lurilee,
Till you sleep in a bramble heap
Or under a gloomy churchyard tree,
And then fly back to swing on a bough,
    Luriana, Lurilee.

CHARLES ELTON

GARDEN SONG

Here in this sequester'd close
Bloom the hyacinth and rose,
Here beside the modest stock
Flaunts the flaring hollyhock;
Here, without a pang, one sees
Ranks, conditions, and degrees.

All the seasons run their race
In this quiet resting-place;
Peach and apricot and fig
Here will ripen and grow big;
Here is store and overplus, –
More had not Alcinoüs!

Here, in alleys cool and green,
Far ahead the thrush is seen;
Here along the southern wall
Keeps the bee his festival;
All is quiet else – afar
Sounds of toil and turmoil are.

Here be shadows large and long;
Here be spaces meet for song;
Grant, O garden-god, that I,
Now that none profane is nigh, –
Now that mood and moment please, –
Find the fair Pierides!

AUSTIN DOBSON

BIRD OF PARADISE

At sunset, only to his true love,
The bird of paradise opened wide his wings
Displaying emerald plumage shot with gold
Unguessed even by him.
                              True, that wide crest
Had blazoned royal estate, and the tropic flowers
Through which he flew had shown example
Of what brave colours gallantry might flaunt,
But these were other. She asked herself, trembling:
'What did I do to awake such glory?'

ROBERT GRAVES

AEGLAMOUR'S LAMENT

Here she was wont to go, and here, and here!
Just where those daisies, pinks, and violets grow:
The world may find the spring by following her;
For other print her airy steps ne'er left:
Her treading would not bend a blade of grass,
Or shake the downy blow-ball from his stalk;
But like the soft west-wind she shot along;
And where she went, the flowers took thickest root
As she had sowed them with her odorous foot.

BEN JONSON

48

MILK FOR THE CAT

When the tea is brought at five o'clock,
And all the neat curtains are drawn with care,
The little black cat with bright green eyes
Is suddenly purring there.

At first she pretends, having nothing to do,
She has come in merely to blink by the grate,
But, though tea may be late or the milk may be sour,
She is never late.

And presently her agate eyes
Take a soft large milky haze,
And her independent casual glance
Becomes a stiff hard gaze.

Then she stamps her claws or lifts her ears
Or twists her tail and begins to stir,
Till suddenly all her lithe body becomes
One breathing trembling purr.

The children eat and wriggle and laugh;
The two old ladies stroke their silk:
But the cat is grown small and thin with desire,
Transformed to a creeping lust for milk.

The white saucer like some full moon descends
At last from the clouds of the table above;
She sighs and dreams and thrills and glows,
Transfigured with love.

She nestles over the shining rim,
Buries her chin in the creamy sea;
Her tail hangs loose; each drowsy paw
Is doubled under each bending knee.

A long dim ecstasy holds her life;
Her world is an infinite shapeless white,
Till her tongue has curled the last holy drop,
Then she sinks back into the night,

Draws and dips her body to heap
Her sleepy nerves in the great arm-chair,
Lies defeated and buried deep
Three or four hours unconscious there.

HAROLD MONRO

A MEMORY

Four ducks on a pond,
A grass bank beyond,
A blue sky of spring,
White clouds on the wing;
What a little thing
To remember for years –
To remember with tears.

WILLIAM ALLINGHAM

TO AUTUMN

Season of mists and mellow fruitfulness,
    Close bosom-friend of the maturing sun;
Conspiring with him how to lead and bless
    With fruit the vines that round the thatch-eaves run;
To bend with apples the moss'd cottage-trees,
    And fill all fruit with ripeness to the core;
      To swell the gourd, and plump the hazel shells
    With a sweet kernel; to set budding more,
And still more, later flowers for the bees,
Until they think warm days will never cease,
      For Summer has o'er-brimm'd their clammy cells.

Who hath not seen thee oft amid thy store?
    Sometimes whoever seeks abroad may find
Thee sitting careless on a granary floor,
    Thy hair soft-lifted by the winnowing wind;
Or on a half-reap'd furrow sound asleep,
      Drowsed with the fume of poppies, while thy hook
      Spares the next swath and all its twinèd flowers;
And sometimes like a gleaner thou dost keep
    Steady thy laden head across a brook;
Or by a cider-press, with patient look,
      Thou watchest the last oozings hours by hours.

Where are the songs of Spring? Ay, where are they?
    Think not of them, thou hast thy music too,
While barred clouds bloom the soft-dying day,
    And touch the stubble-plains with rosy hue;
Then in a wilful choir the small gnats mourn
    Among the river sallows, borne aloft
      Or sinking as the light wind lives or dies;
And full-grown lambs loud bleat from hilly bourn;
Hedge-crickets sing; and now with treble soft
The redbreast whistles from a garden-croft;
      And gathering swallows twitter in the skies.

JOHN KEATS

ABUNDANCE

Africanus meant
the conqueror sent
    from Rome. It should mean the
    Untouched: the sand-brown jumping-rat – free-born; and
    the blacks, that choice race with an elegance
    ignored by one's ignorance.

Part terrestrial,
and part celestial,
    Jacob saw, cudgel staff
    in claw-hand – steps of air and air angels; his
    friends were the stones. The translucent mistake
    of the desert, does not make

hardship for one who
can rest and then do
    the opposite – launching
    as if on wings, from its match-thin hind legs, in
    daytime or at night; that departs with great
    speed, followed by, as a weight,

a double length, thin
tail furred like the skin;
    that curls round it when it
    sleeps 'round' – the nose nested in fur, a hind leg
    at each side of the head – or lies lengthwise,
    in view, when the body lies

flat. Seen by daylight,
the body is white
    in front; and on the back,
    buffy-brown like the breast of the fawn-breasted
    bower-bird. It hops like the fawn-breast, but has
    chipmunk contours – perceived as

it turns its bird head —
the nap directed
      neatly back and blending
      with the ear which reiterates the slimness
      of the body. The fine hairs on the tail,
      repeating the other pale

markings, lengthen till
at the tip they fill
      out in a tuft — black and
      white; strange detail of the simplified creature,
      fish-shaped and silvered to steel by the force
      of the large desert moon. Course

the jerboa, or
plunder its food store,
      and you will be cursed. It
      honours the sand by assuming its colour;
      closed upper paws seeming one with the fur
      in its flight from a danger.

By fifths and sevenths,
in leaps of two lengths,
      like the uneven notes
      of the Bedouin flute, it stops its gleaning
      on little wheel castors, and makes fern-seed
      foot-prints with kangaroo speed.

Its leaps should be set
to the flageolet;
      pillar body erect
      on a three-cornered smooth-working Chippendale
      claw — propped on hind legs, and tail as third toe,
      between leaps to its burrow.

MARIANNE MOORE

SONG

The feathers of the willow
Are half of them grown yellow
    Above the swelling stream;
And ragged are the bushes,
And rusty now the rushes,
    And wild the clouded gleam.

The thistle now is older,
His stalk begins to moulder,
    His head is white as snow;
The branches all are barer,
The linnet's song is rarer,
    The robin pipeth now.

R. W. DIXON

A WIDOW BIRD SATE MOURNING

A widow bird sate mourning for her love
    Upon a wintry bough;
The frozen wind crept on above,
    The freezing stream below.

There was no leaf upon the forest bare,
    No flower upon the ground,
And little motion in the air
    Except the mill-wheel's sound.

PERCY BYSSHE SHELLEY

THE PASSIONATE SHEPHERD TO HIS LOVE

Come live with me and be my Love,
And we will all the pleasures prove
That hills and valleys, dales and fields,
Or woods or steepy mountain yields.

And we will sit upon the rocks,
And see the shepherds feed their flocks
By shallow rivers, to whose falls
Melodious birds sing madrigals.

And I will make thee beds of roses
And a thousand fragrant posies;
A cap of flowers, and a kirtle
Embroider'd all with leaves of myrtle.

A gown made of the finest wool
Which from our pretty lambs we pull;
Fair-lined slippers for the cold,
With buckles of the purest gold.

A belt of straw and ivy-buds
With coral clasps and amber studs:
And if these pleasures may thee move,
Come live with me and be my Love.

The shepherd swains shall dance and sing
For thy delight each May morning:
If these delights thy mind may move,
Then live with me and be my Love.

CHRISTOPHER MARLOWE

AH! SUN-FLOWER

Ah, Sun-flower! weary of time,
Who countest the steps of the sun;
Seeking after that sweet golden clime,
Where the traveller's journey is done;

Where the Youth pined away with desire,
And the pale Virgin shrouded in snow,
Arise from their graves, and aspire
Where my Sun-flower wishes to go.

WILLIAM BLAKE

THE SADNESS OF THINGS FOR SAPPHO'S SICKNESS

Lilies will languish; violets look ill,
Sickly the primrose; pale the daffodil;
That gallant tulip will hang down his head,
Like to a virgin newly ravished;
Pansies will weep, and marigolds will wither,
And keep a fast and funeral together;
If Sappho droop, daisies will open never,
But bid good-night, and close their lids for ever.

ROBERT HERRICK

UT IN THE DARK

Out in the dark over the snow
The fallow fawns invisible go
With the fallow doe;
And the winds blow
Fast as the stars are slow.

Stealthily the dark haunts round
And, when the lamp goes, without sound
At a swifter bound
Than the swiftest hound,
Arrives, and all else is drowned;

And I and star and wind and deer,
Are in the dark together, – near,
Yet far, – and fear
Drums on my ear
In that sage company drear.

How weak and little is the light,
All the universe of sight,
Love and delight,
Before the might,
If you love it not, of night.

EDWARD THOMAS

SONG

A spirit haunts the year's last hours
Dwelling amid these yellowing bowers:
      To himself he talks;
For at eventide, listening earnestly,
At his work you may hear him sob and sigh
      In the walks;
      Earthward he boweth the heavy stalks
Of the mouldering flowers:
   Heavily hangs the broad sunflower
      Over its grave i' the earth so chilly;
Heavily hangs the hollyhock,
      Heavily hangs the tiger-lily.

The air is damp, and hush'd, and close
As a sick man's room when he taketh repose
      An hour before death;
My very heart faints and my whole soul grieves
At the moist rich smell of the rotting leaves,
      And the breath
      Of the fading edges of box beneath,
And the year's last rose.
   Heavily hangs the broad sunflower
      Over its grave i' the earth so chilly;
   Heavily hangs the hollyhock,
      Heavily hangs the tiger-lily.

ALFRED TENNYSON

Grateful thanks are due to the following for kind
permission to reprint the copyright poems
in this volume:

A. D. Peters & Co. for the poem by Edmund
Blunden; the Estate of Robert Frost, Jonathan
Cape Ltd. and Holt, Rinehart & Winston, Inc. for
the poem from *The Poetry of Robert Frost*: Edited by
Edward Connery Lathem; Robert Graves for the
poem from his *Collected Poems 1975*; Faber & Faber
Ltd and The Macmillan Company for the poem
from *The Complete Poems of Marianne Moore*.
Copyright 1935 by Marianne Moore, renewed 1963
by Marianne Moore and T. S. Eliot; Harper &
Row, Publishers, Inc. for the poem by E. B. White
from *The Second Tree from the Corner*. Copyright 1952
by E. B. White. Originally appeared in
The New Yorker.